SKETCH BOOK FOR YOUR DESIGN
INTERIOR DESIGN AND DECORATE
SKETCH BOOK

Volume #1

By

Nontvaris

SKETCH BOOK FOR YOUR DESIGN
INTERIOR DESIGN AND DECORATE
SKETCH BOOK

Volume #1

Copyright: Published in the United States by Nontvaris
Published july2016

ISBN-13: 978-1536813692
ISBN-10: 1536813699

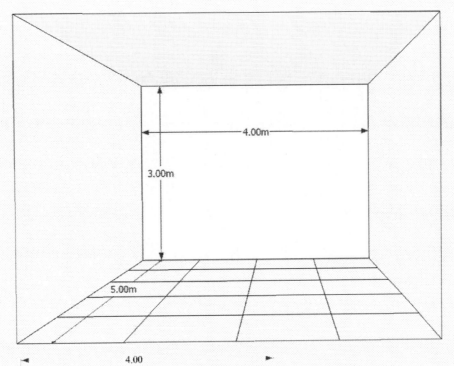

4.00m

3.00m

5.00m

4.00

5.00

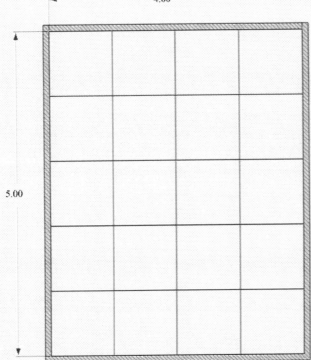

For your decorate
Room size W4xL5xH3 meter

. . . .

. . . .

. . . .

. . . .

. . . .

. . . .

. . . .

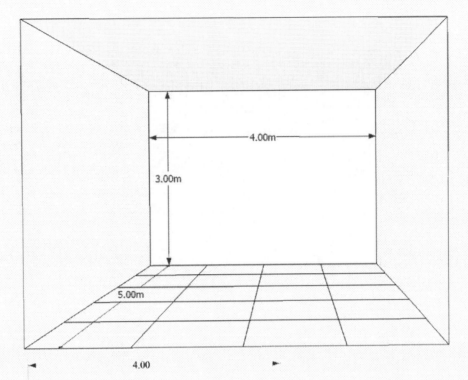

4.00m

3.00m

5.00m

4.00

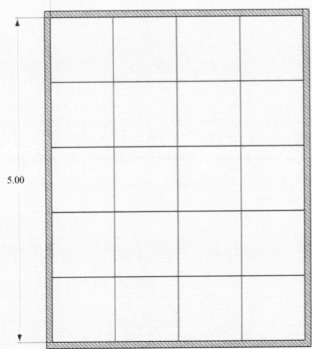

5.00

For your decorate
Room size W4xL5xH3 meter

. . . .

. . . .

. . . .

. . . .

. . . .

. . . .

. . . .

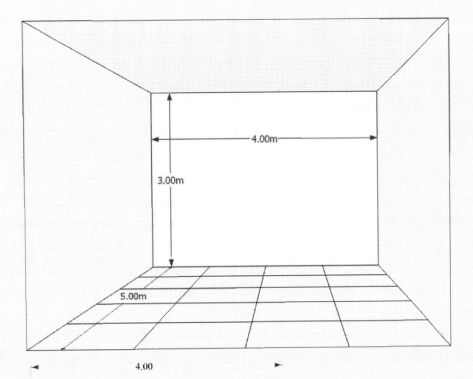

4.00m

3.00m

5.00m

4.00

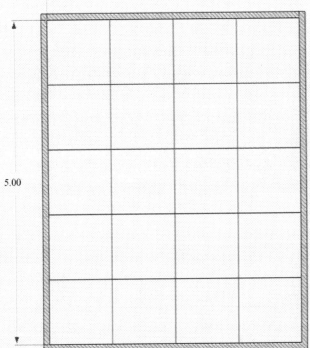

5.00

For your decorate
Room size W4xL5xH3 meter

....
....
....
....
....
....
....
....

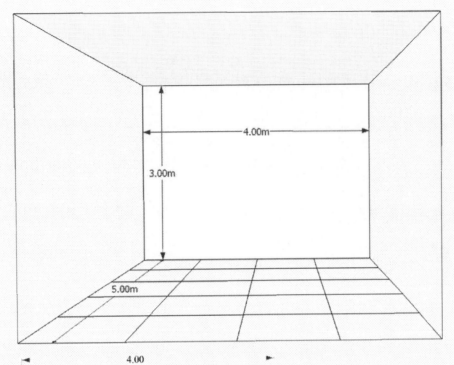

4.00m

3.00m

5.00m

4.00

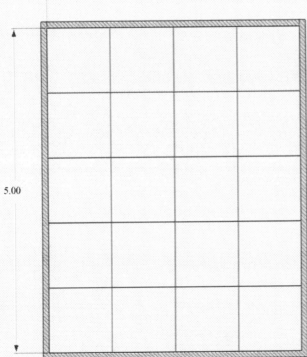

5.00

For your decorate
Room size W4xL5xH3 meter

. . . .

. . . .

. . . .

. . . .

. . . .

. . . .

. . . .

. . . .

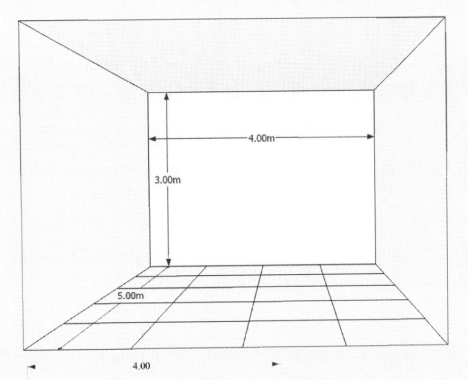

4.00m

3.00m

5.00m

4.00

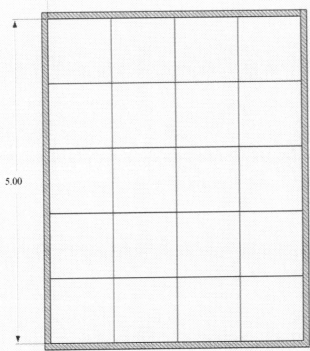

5.00

For your decorate
Room size W4xL5xH3 meter

. . . .
. . . .
. . . .
. . . .
. . . .
. . . .
. . . .

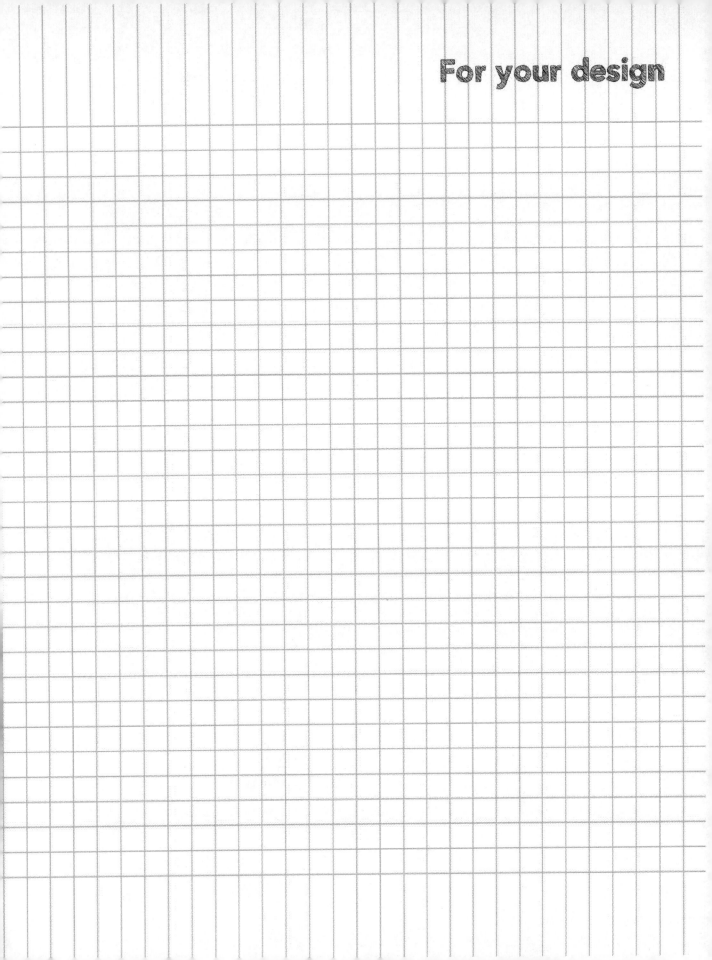

For your design

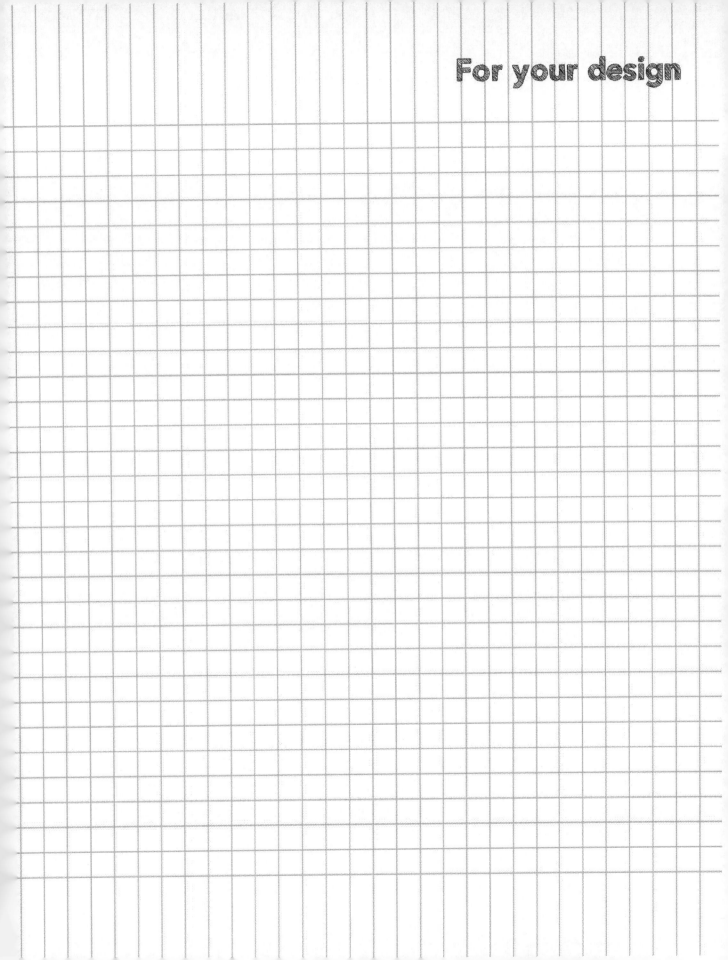
For your design

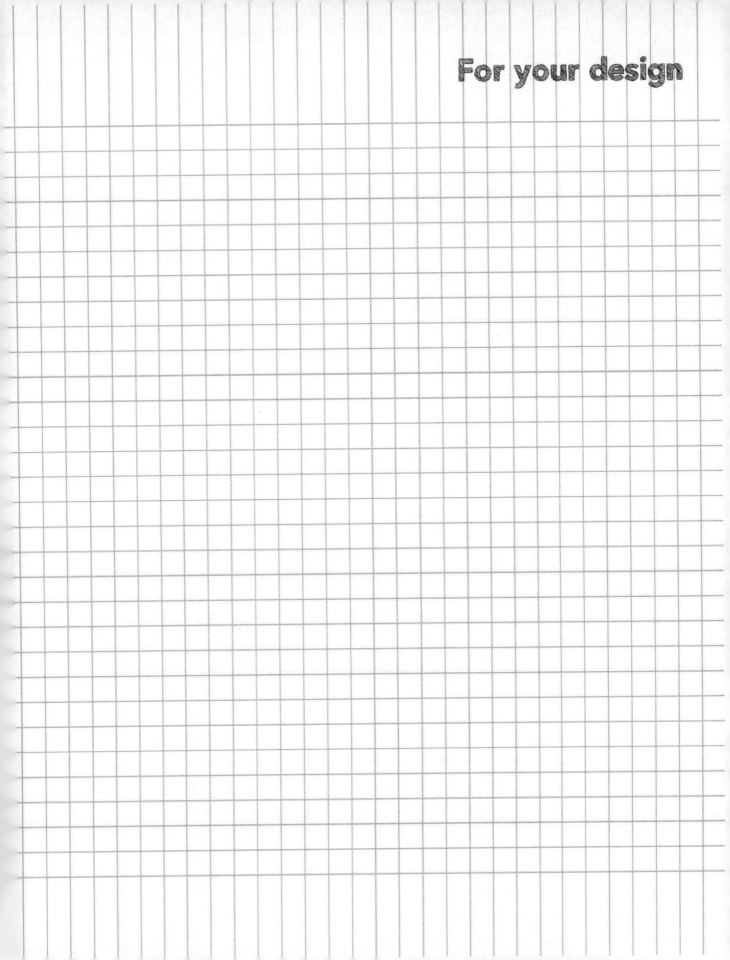

For your design

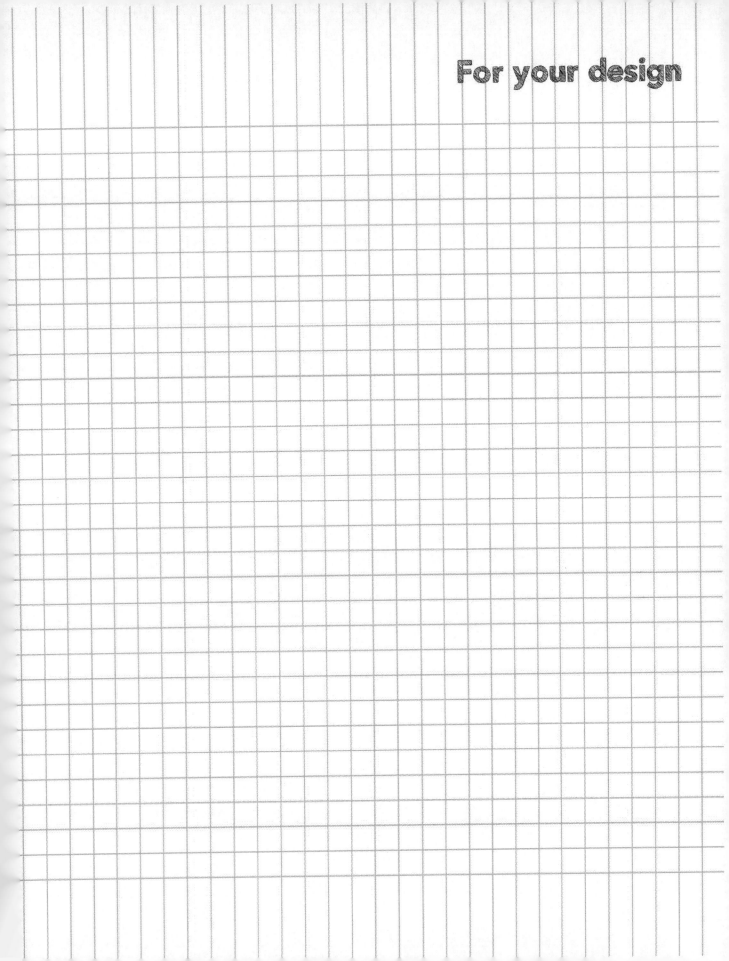

For your design

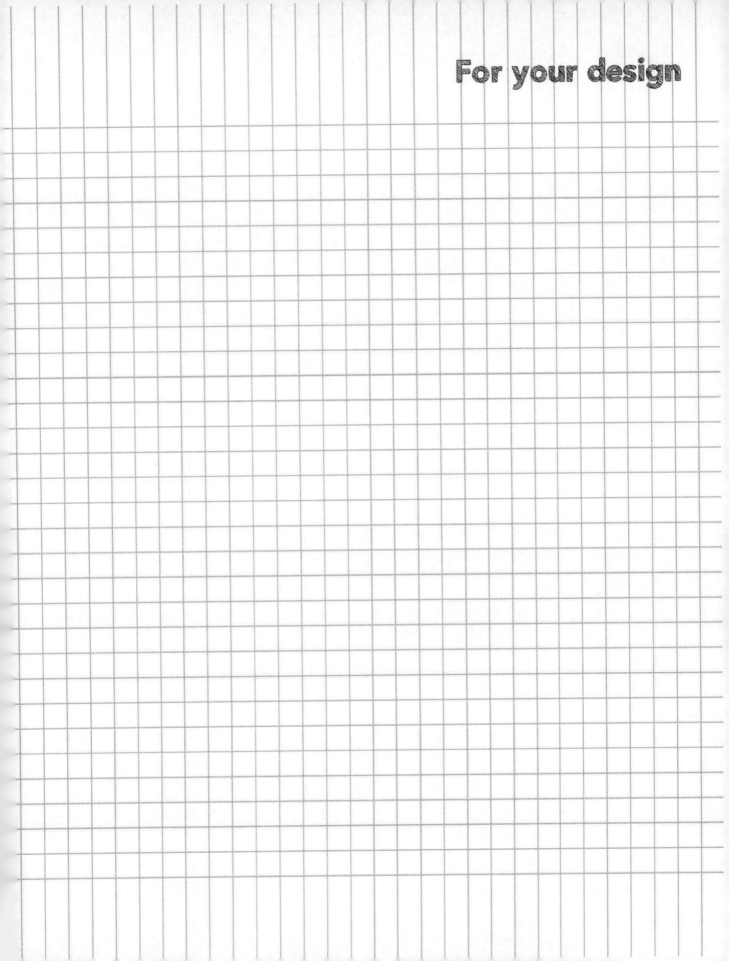

For your design

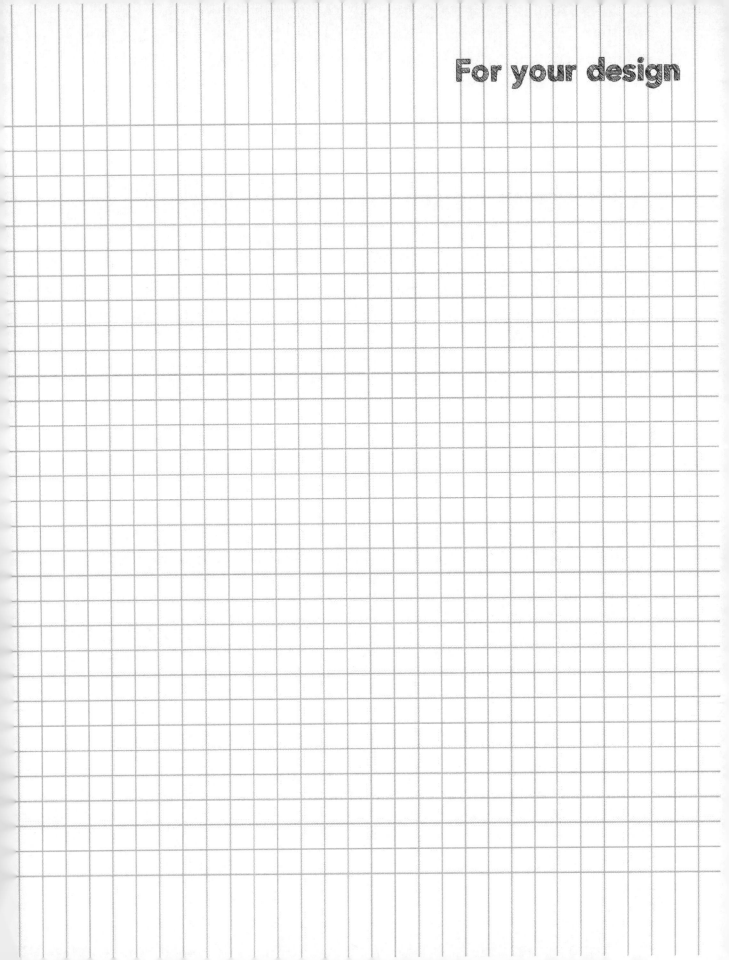

For your design

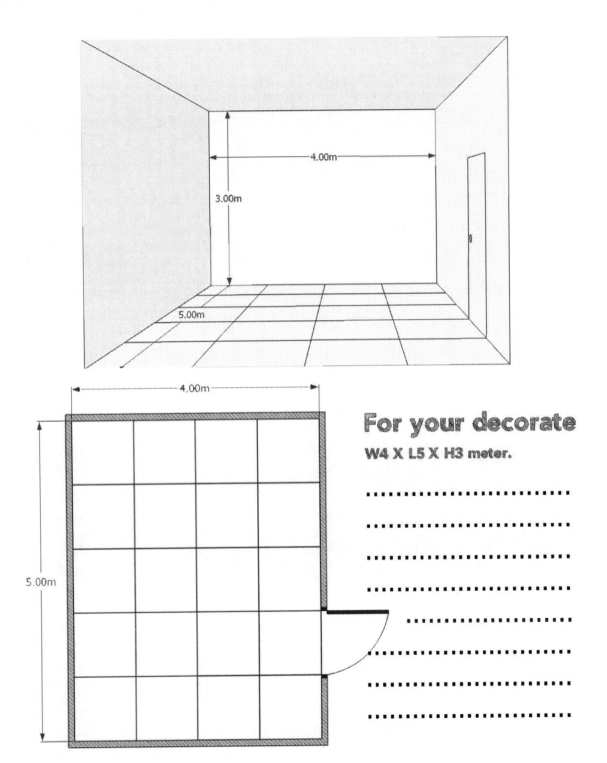

For your decorate

W4 X L5 X H3 meter.

....

....

....

....

....

....

....

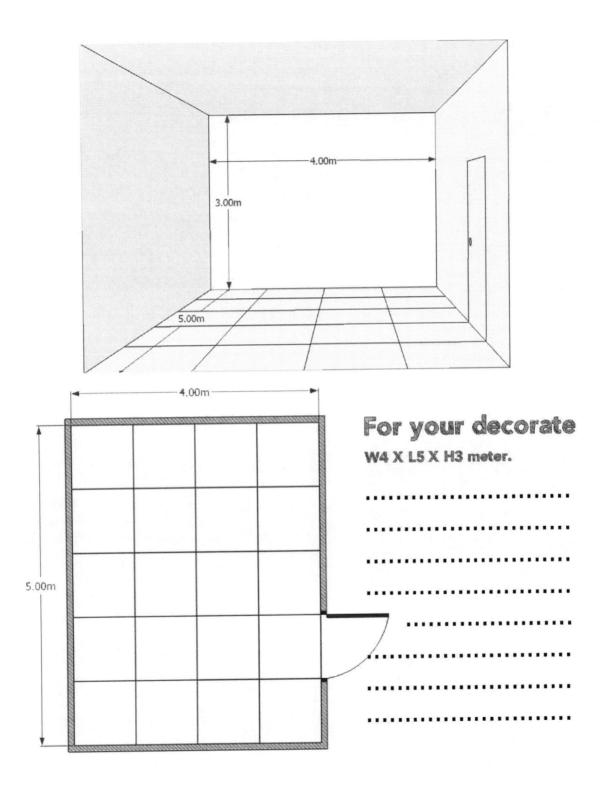

For your decorate
W4 X L5 X H3 meter.

....
....
....
....
....
....
....
....

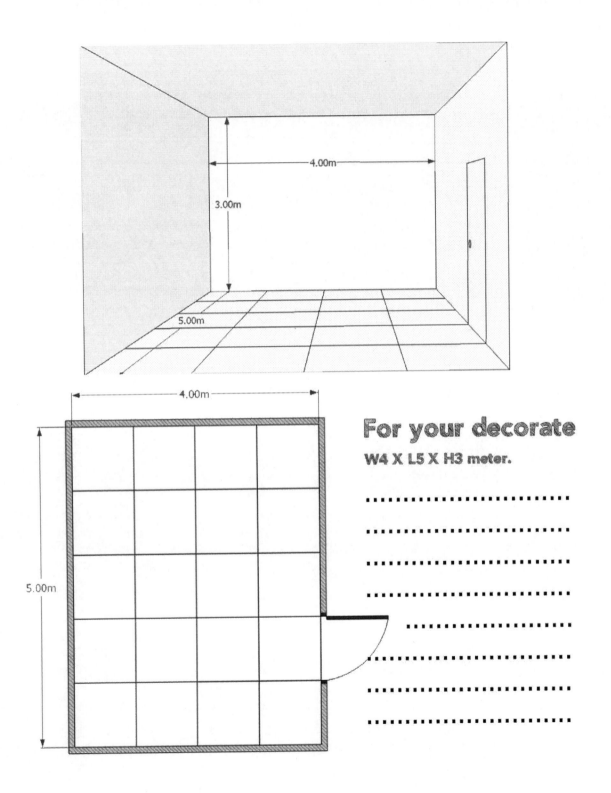

For your decorate

W4 X L5 X H3 meter.

....
....
....
....
....
....
....
....

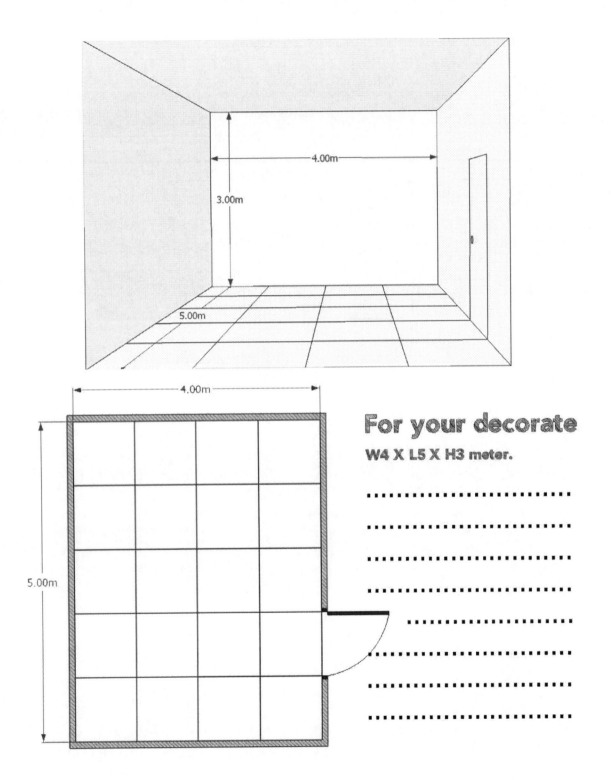

4.00m

3.00m

5.00m

4.00m

5.00m

For your decorate
W4 X L5 X H3 meter.

....

....

....

....

....

....

....

....

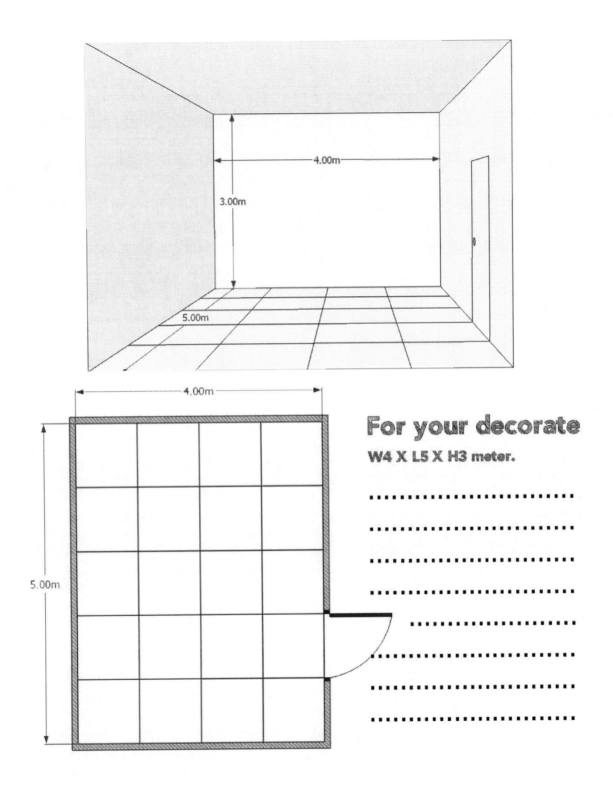

4.00m

3.00m

5.00m

4.00m

5.00m

For your decorate
W4 X L5 X H3 meter.

······························
······························
······························
······························
  ··························
   ·························
     ·······················
      ······················

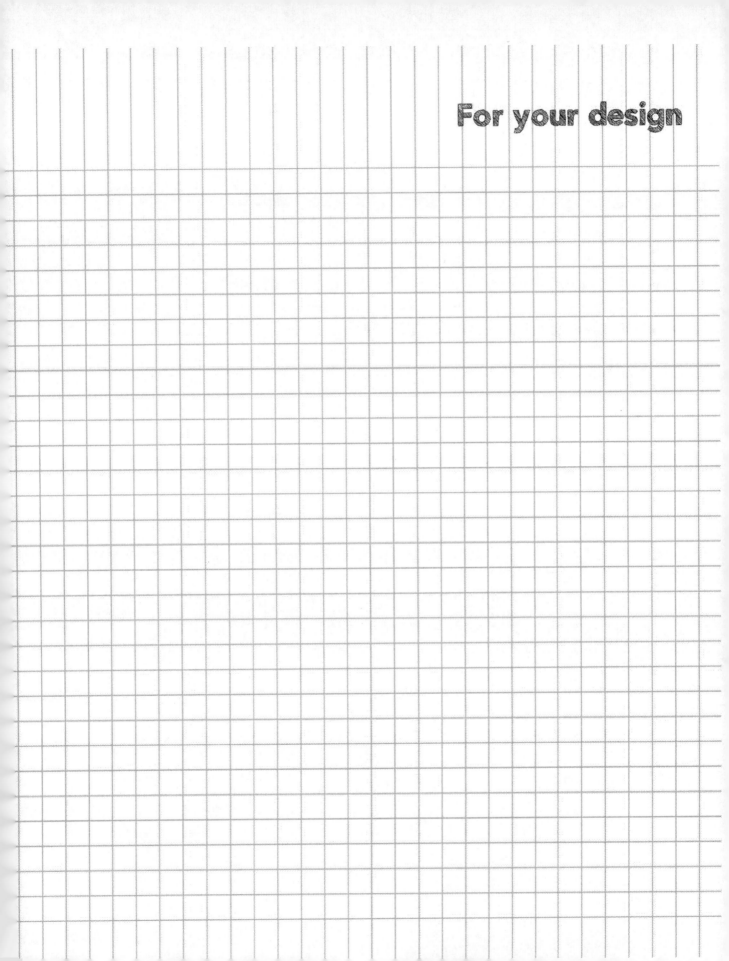

For your design

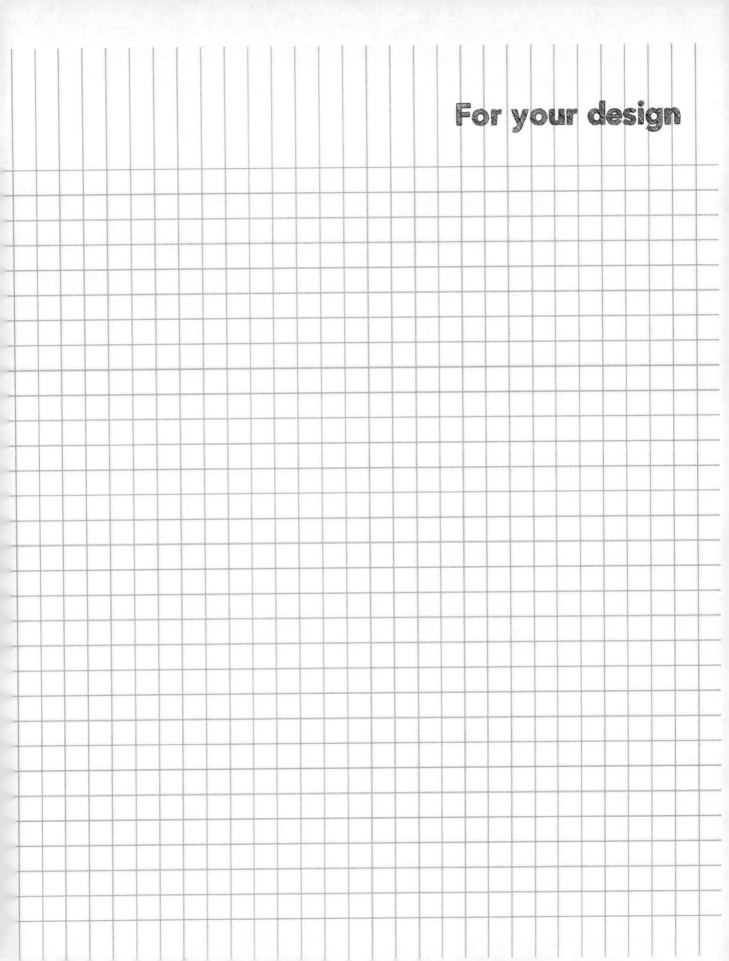

For your design

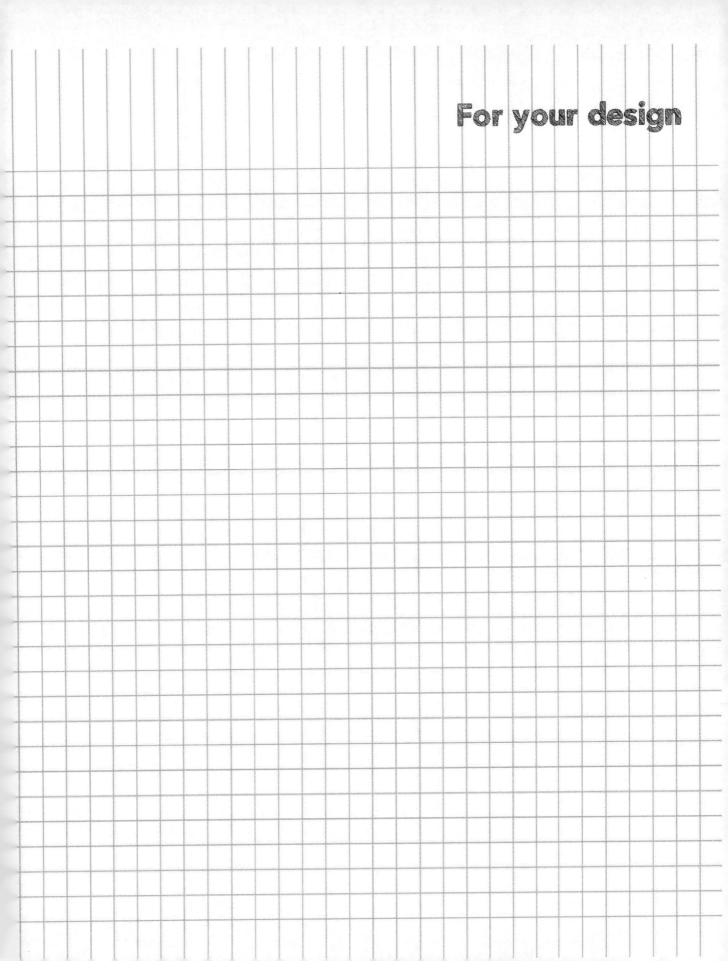

For your design

For your design

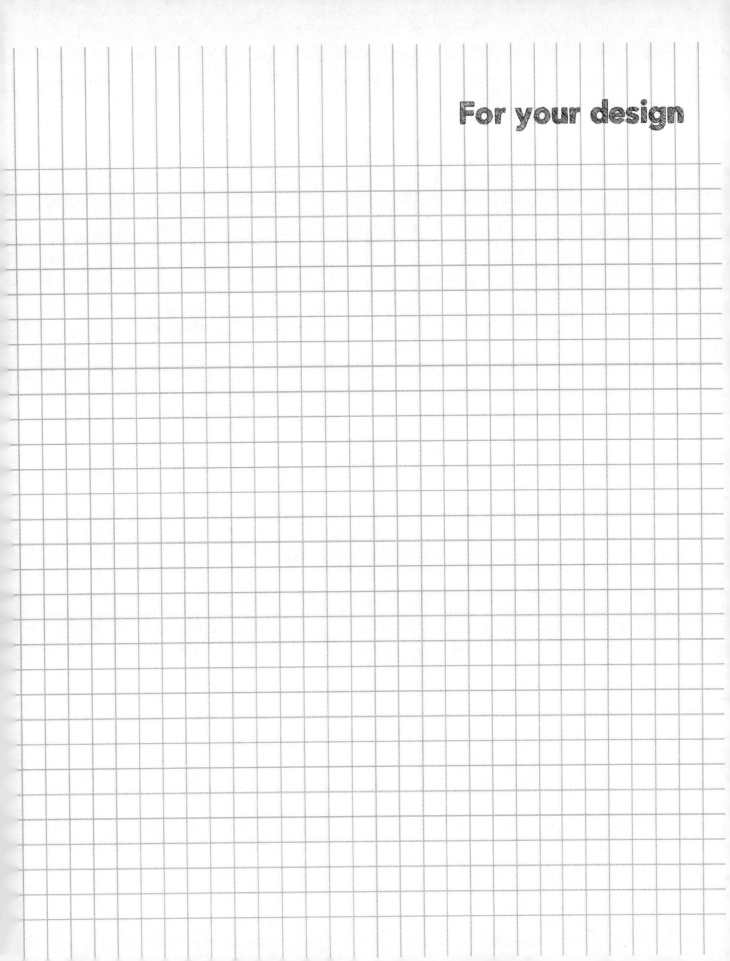

For your design

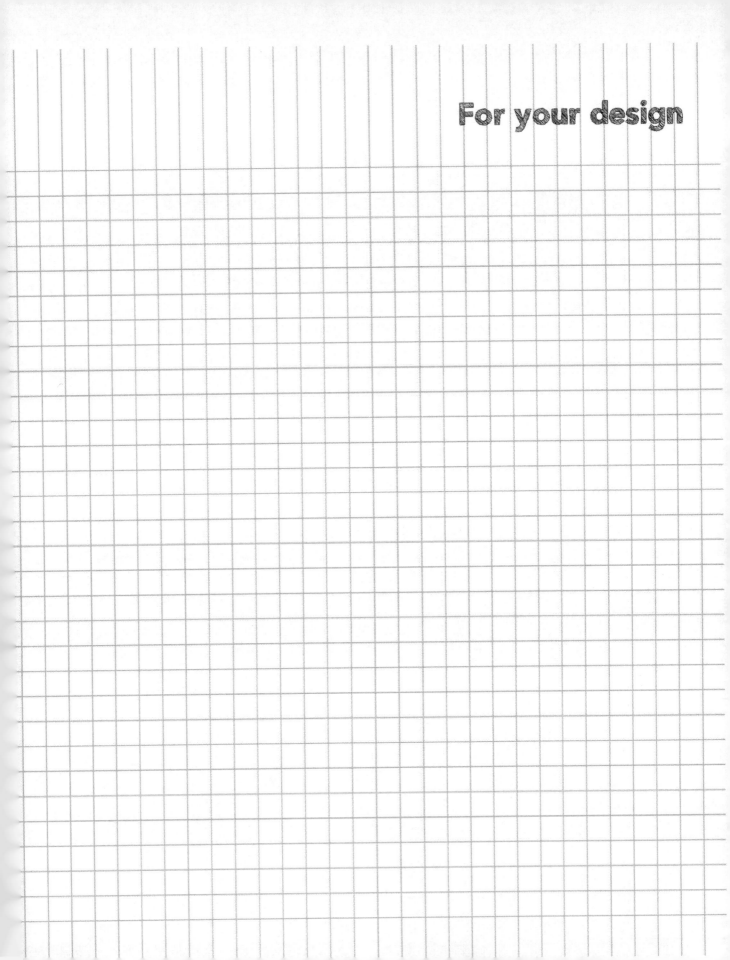

For your design

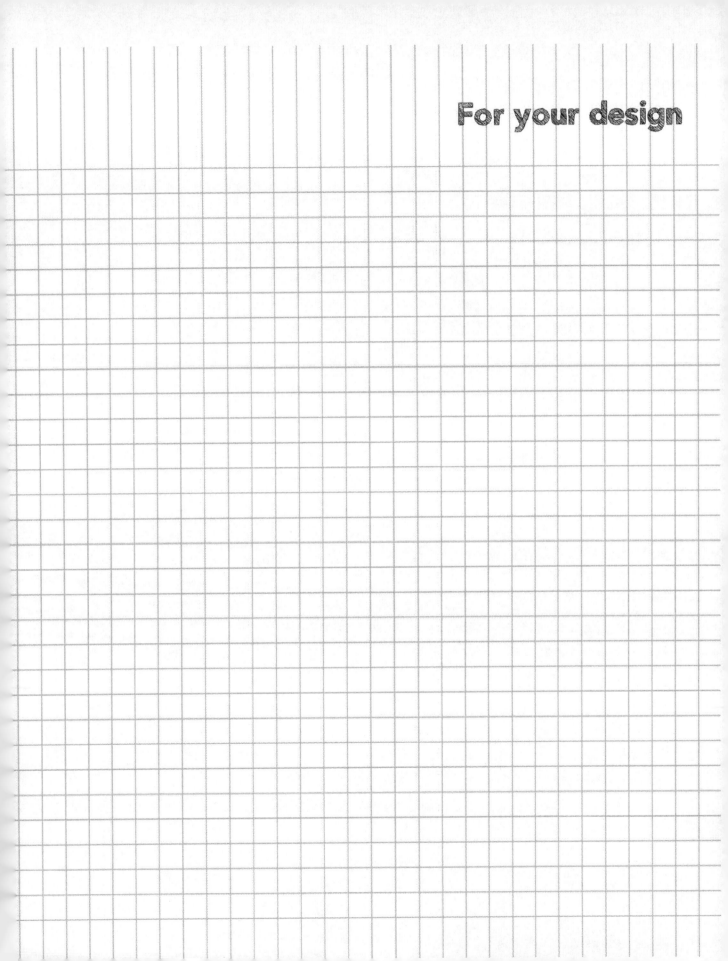

For your design

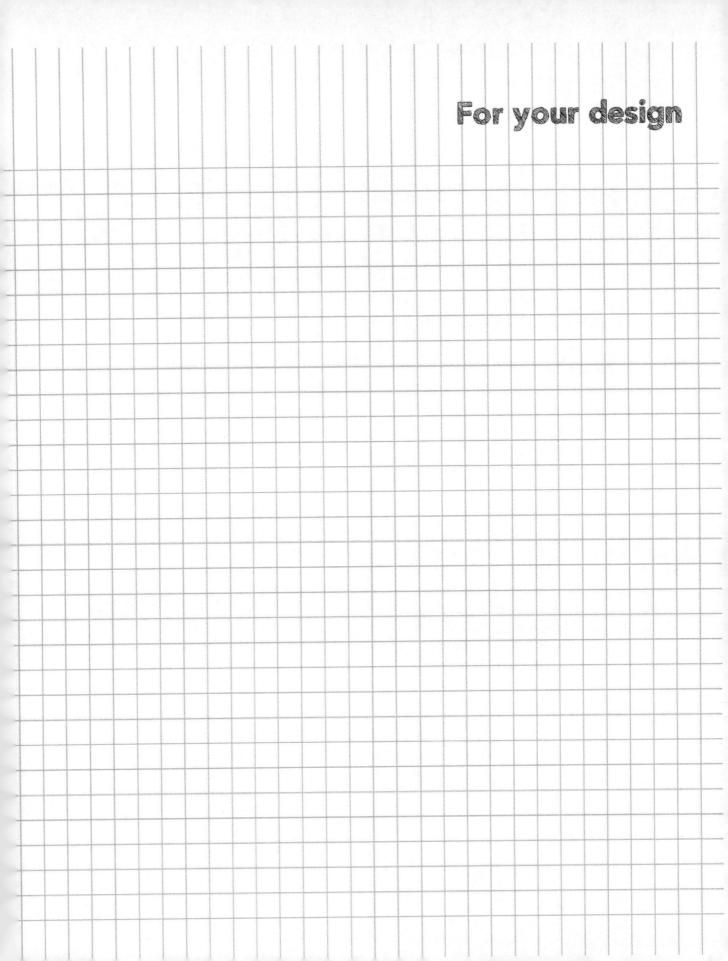

For your design

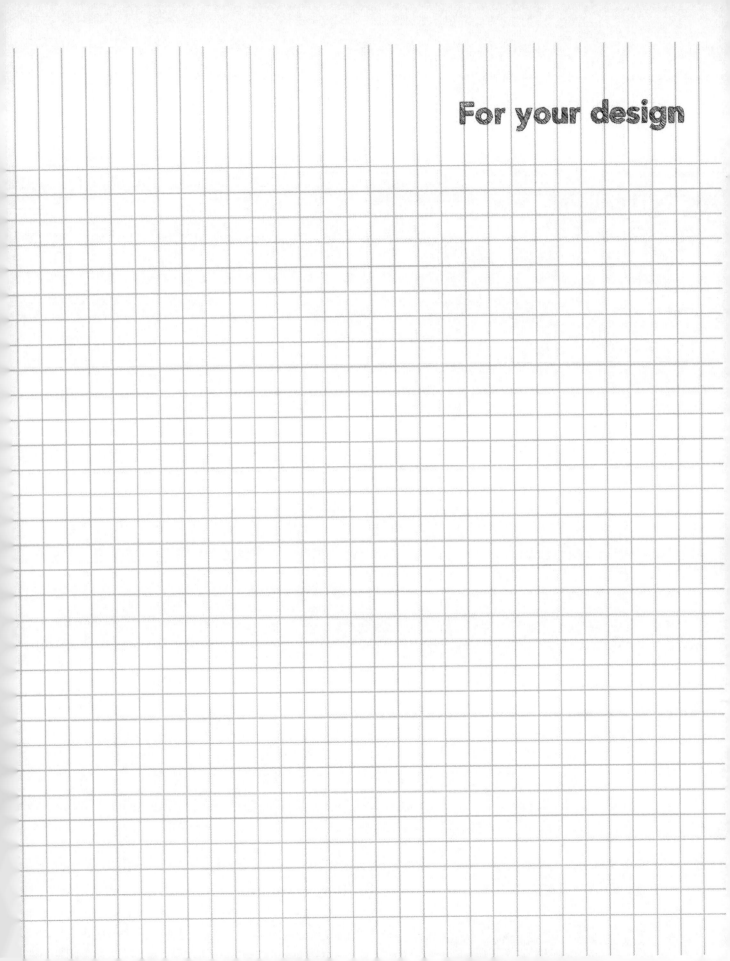

For your design

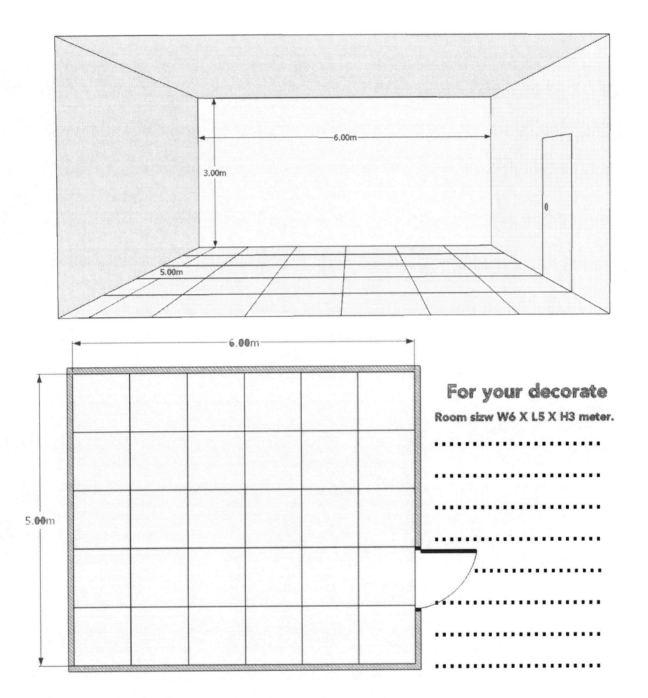

For your decorate

Room sizw W6 X L5 X H3 meter.

. . . .

. . . .

. . . .

. . . .

. . . .

. . . .

. . . .

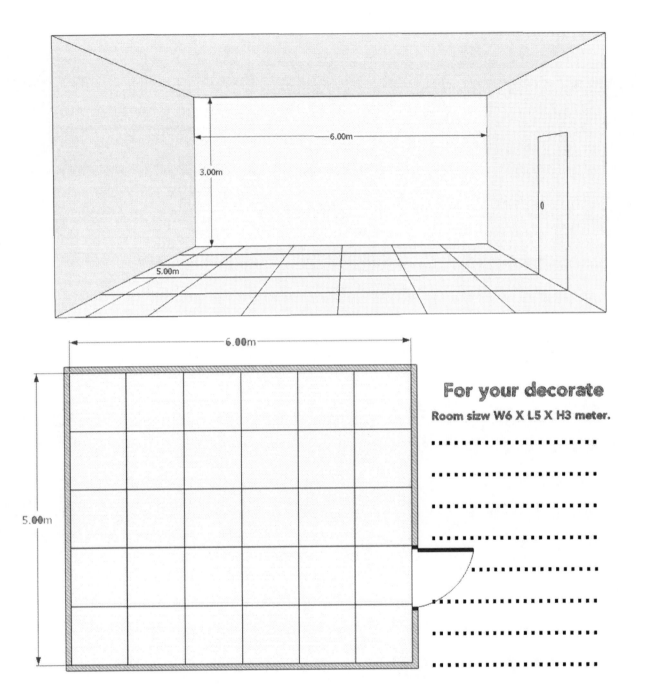

For your decorate

Room sizw W6 X L5 X H3 meter.

....

....

....

....

....

....

....

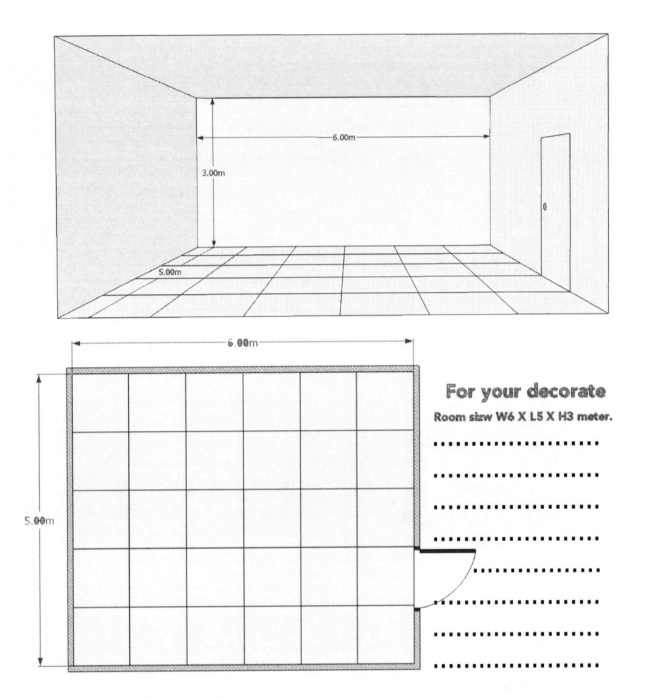

For your decorate

Room sizw W6 X L5 X H3 meter.

....
....
....
....
....
....
....

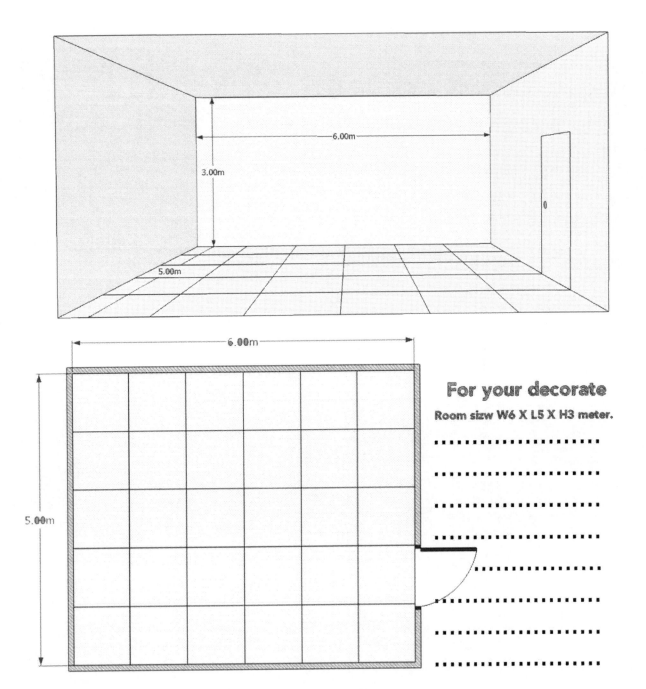

For your decorate

Room sizw W6 X L5 X H3 meter.

....

....

....

....

....

....

....

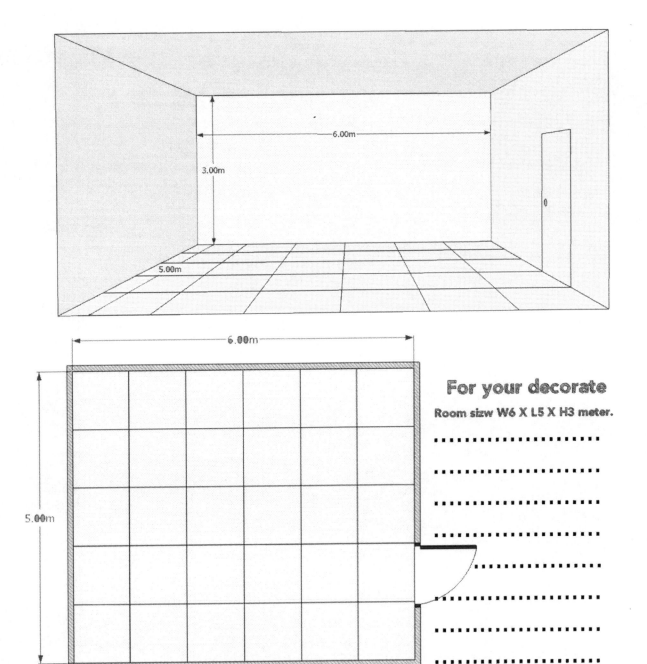

6.00m

3.00m

5.00m

6.00m

5.00m

For your decorate

Room sizw W6 X L5 X H3 meter.

....
....
....
....
....
....
....

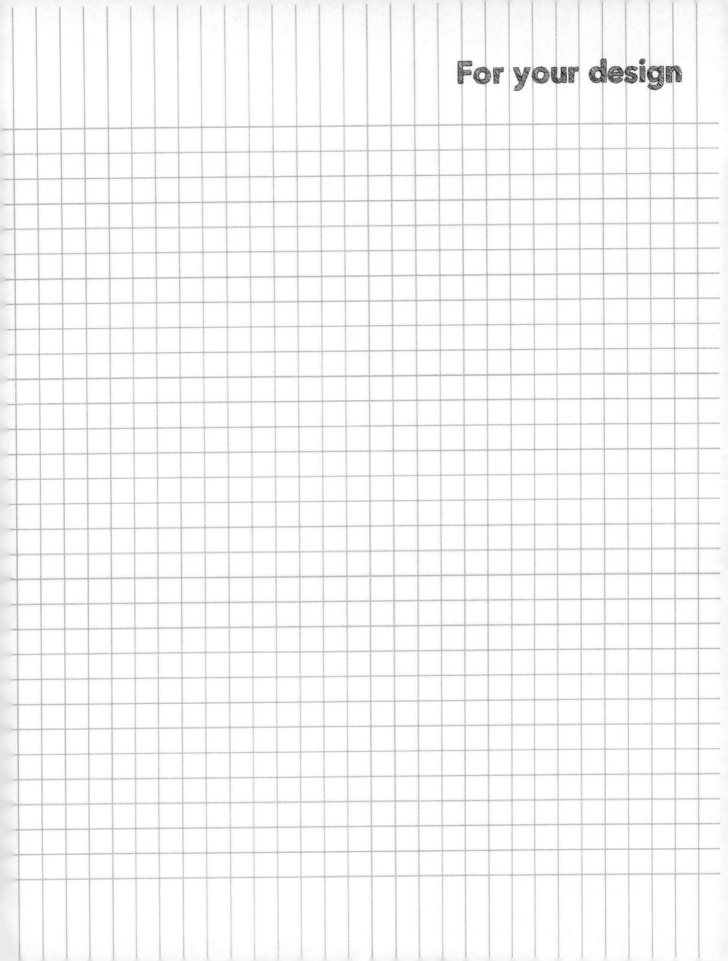

For your design

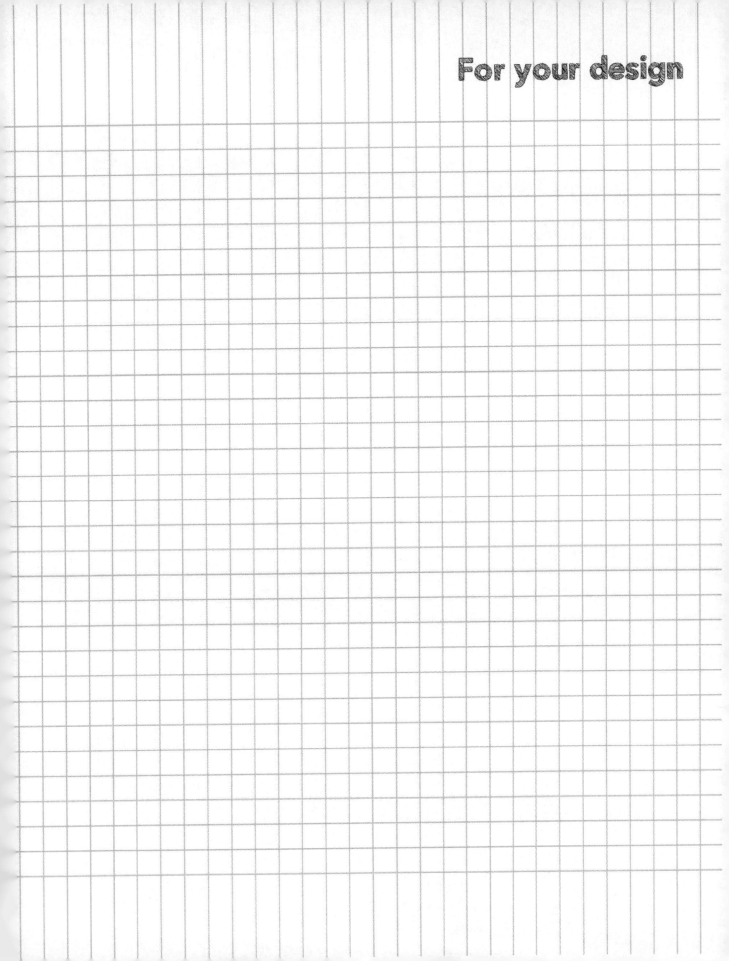

For your design

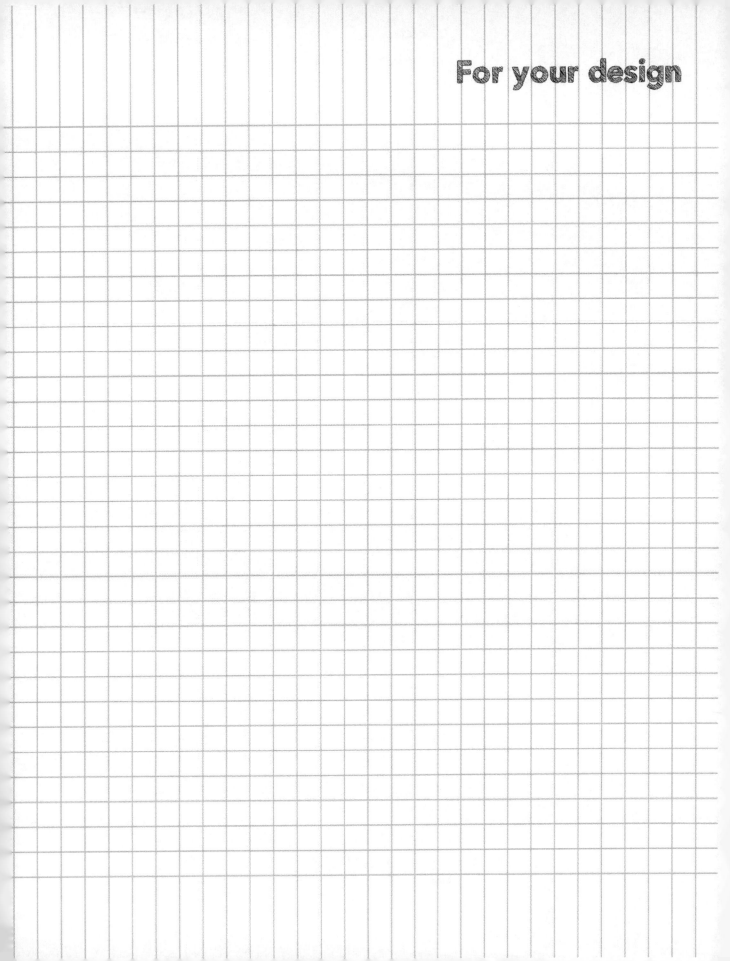

For your design

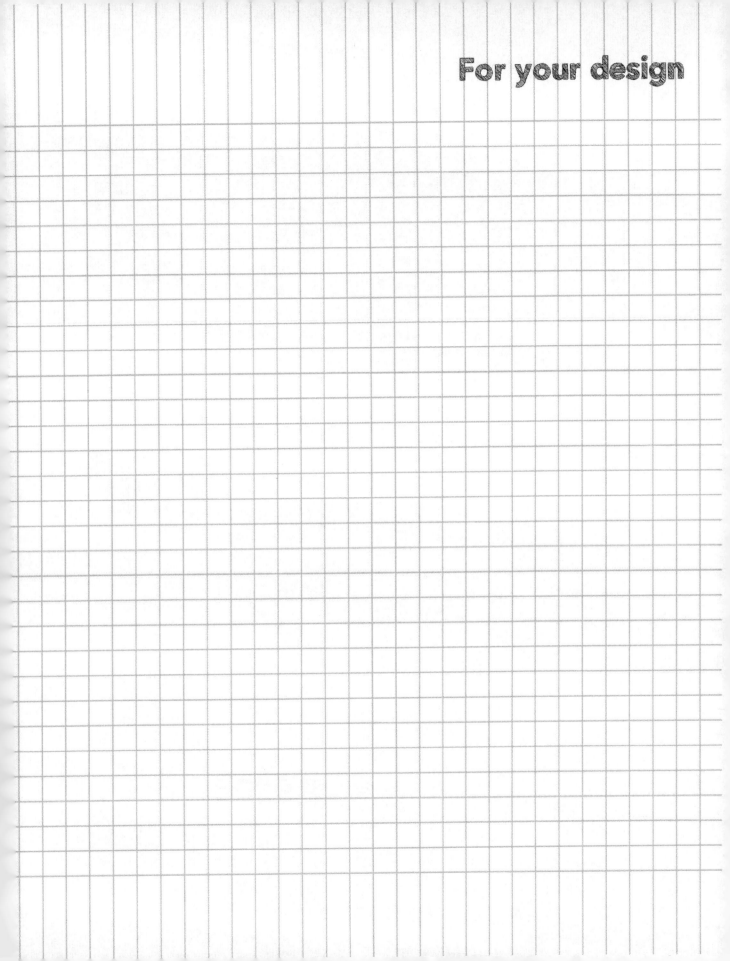

For your design

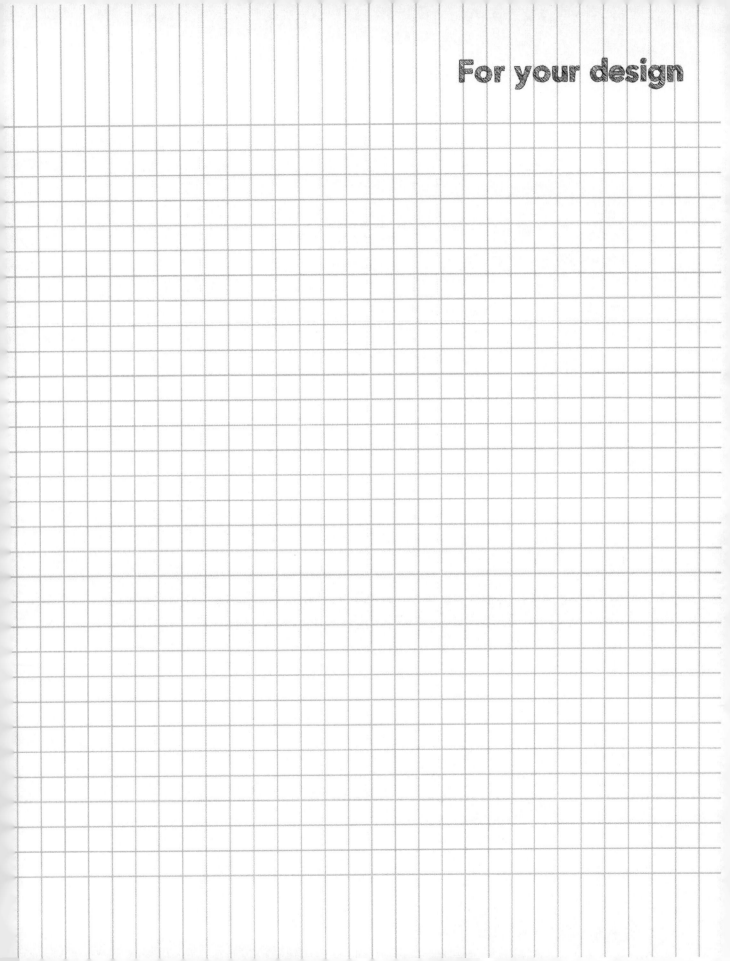

For your design

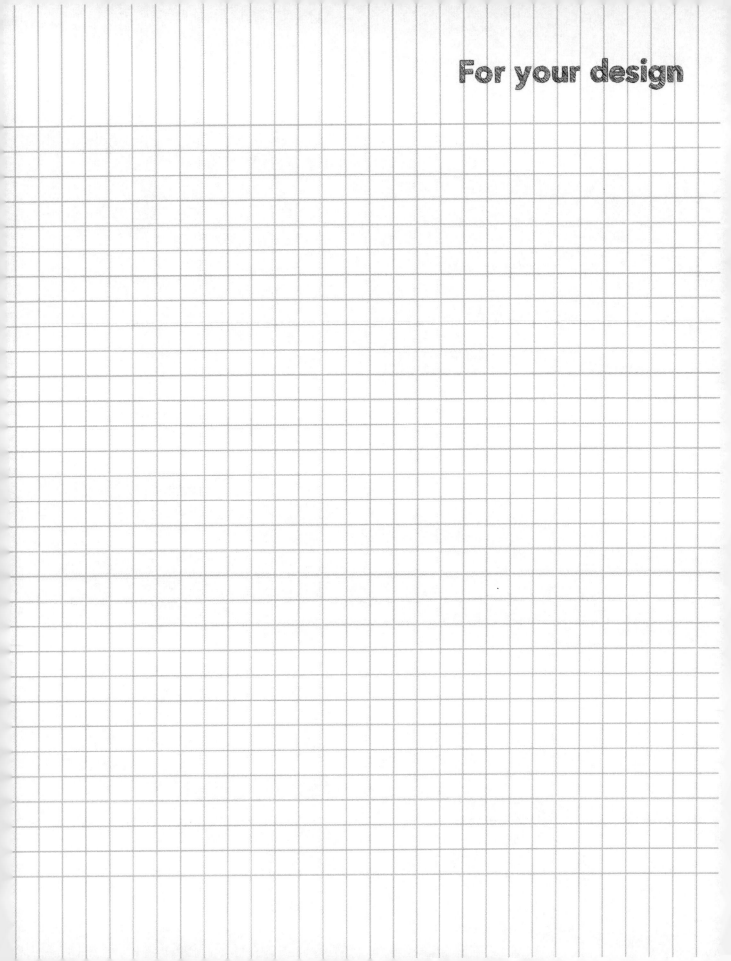

For your design

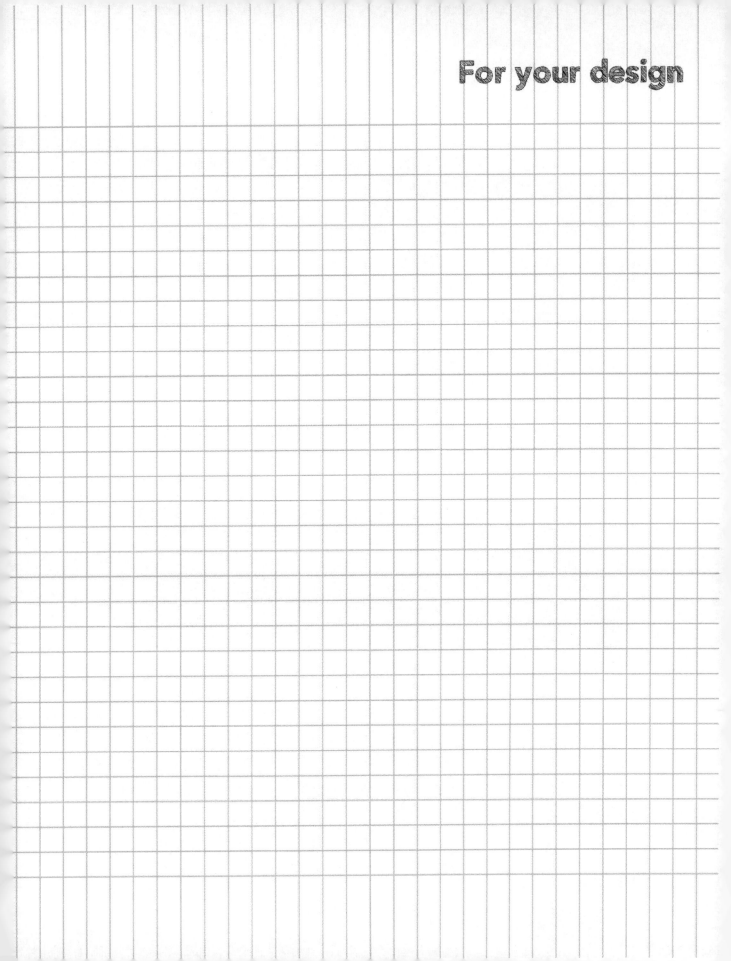

For your design

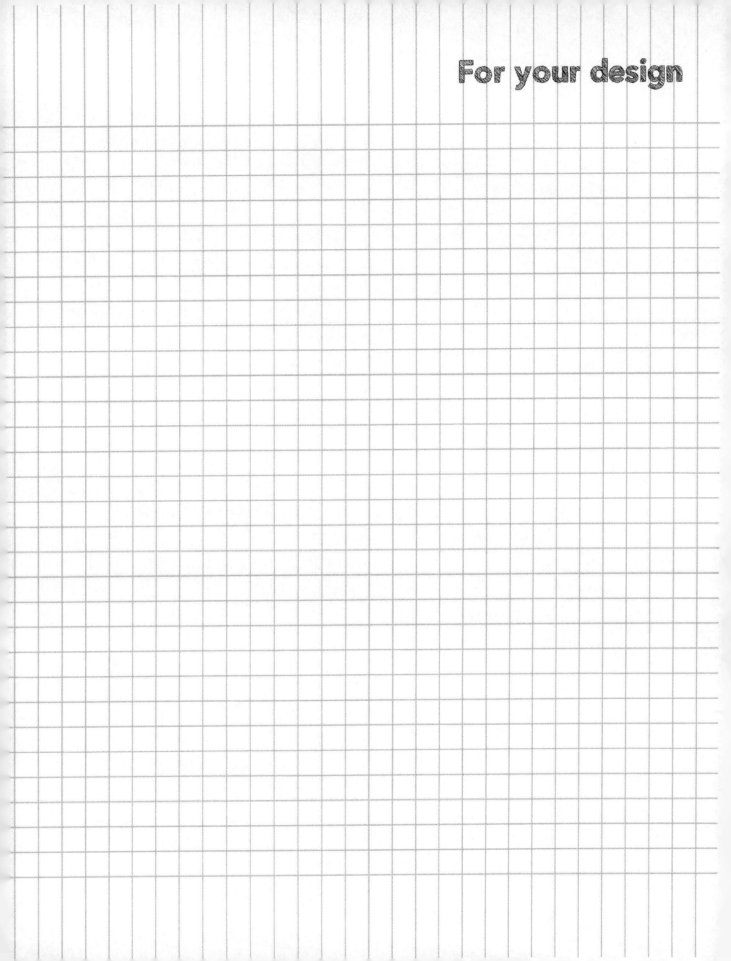

For your design

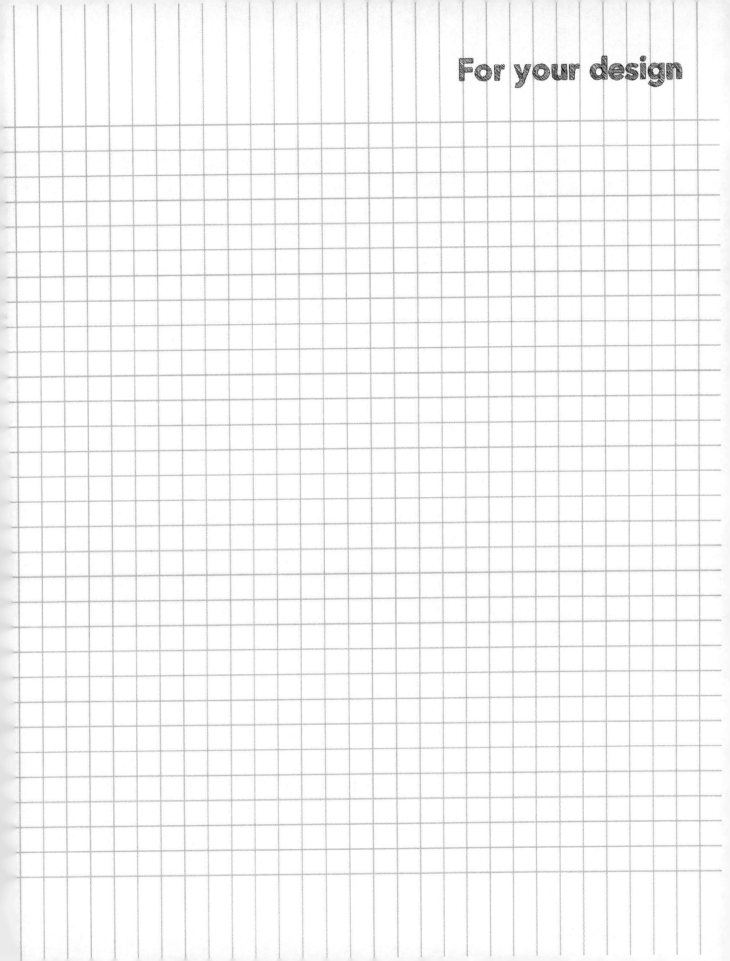

For your design

For your design

Thank you

Made in the USA
Middletown, DE
01 December 2019